In Pursuit

Coaching Orals

Plan – Prepare – Practice - Present

Enabling Business

To Win Business

Like Big Business

Mike Rice

In Pursuit – Coaching Orals

A Business Development Life Cycle Companion Topic

ISBN: 9781088943502

Publisher: CornerStone IT, LLC
Author: Mike Rice
Series: In Pursuit

CornerStone IT, LLC
Email: InPursuit@CornerStoneIT-llc.com

Table of Contents

Preface

This adventure began with In Pursuit – A Business Development Life Cycle. At one point, I had a full chapter written on the "4 P's" of Orals Coaching. I was struggling with how to get other topics within the framework of the Life Cycle expressed without the original book ending up being 500 pages thick. A good friend of mine and a well-respected capture pro suggested that I keep the Life Cycle pure and create smaller companion topical books as part of the In Pursuit series. This the first of those companion books.

As a teacher, I enjoy sharing what I've studied and prepared for. There is a sense of accomplishment when a student or someone in the audience "gets it". I've coached competitive sports my entire adult life. There is that same sense of satisfaction when one of the players overcomes some hinderance in their performance and exceeds their own expectations as a competitor.

Reflection: Player development takes a lot of hard work for both the training staff and the individual player. As a coach I've had moments of frustration; but so, did the player. When a player makes a mistake, a good coach understands the value of mercy, graciously corrects the mistake and encourages their young protégé to continue to do their best. Most competitive players long to see their own good fruit. There is no greater feeling then to encourage the transformation of that player into a competitive machine; one who is comfortable in their ability to produce. I need to brag on one of my players (who is also my son). Incredible at the sweeper position in soccer, Aaron was also a talented hockey defenseman. Aaron was fast as lighting on skates and could pickpocket the puck from anyone within his reach. His weakness, though, was his slapshot; falling back on a wrist shot when giving the opportunity to shoot. The coaching staff was working with and encouraging Aaron; he had every other skill needed to be an offensive threat too. One practice, early in the season, we heard what sounded like a gunshot from the rink. We looked up and saw that it was Aaron. Slapshot after slapshot on net; each one with as much heat as the last. The coaching staff and team just watched in amazement. One of the coaches hollered, "Hey Aaron, where did that come from"? He responded with a smile, "I finally figured it out, Coach!" After all that encouragement, Aaron transformed into that threat everyone knew he could be. By the way, that team, that year, went on to win a national championship for their age group!

I've participated in and coached oral presentations over the past twenty years. The most profound qualities I have learned from those coaching experiences are that a coach must have an appreciation for the anatomy of the game; then plan, prepare, and practice to foster excellence within the team and ensure high percentages of wins. Elite coaches must know the mechanics of the game and plan to execute within its boundaries. They must understand each player and prepare them for their role or position on the team. The coach must develop the team's dynamics, practicing the team such that their performance is consistent and automatic. Finally, a highly effective coach has a game plan; at game time, execute the game plan, and there are very little surprises.

Introduction

FAR 15.102[1] states, "(a) Oral presentations by offerors as requested by the Government **may substitute for, or augment, written information**. Use of oral presentations as a substitute for portions of a proposal can be effective in **streamlining the source selection process.**" 15.102 (a) continues "Oral presentations provide an **opportunity for dialogue among the parties**. Pre-recorded videotaped presentations that lack real-time interactive dialogue are not considered oral presentations for the purposes of this section, although they may be included in offeror submissions, when appropriate."

I appreciate the latitude the FAR gives the Acquisition team in leveraging the Oral presentation platform. Note the bolds above. Orals can replace written material; they are designed to streamline source selection and encourages two-way communications between the agency and industry. Also note that recorded video presentation is not considered an Oral presentation, due to the lack of interactive dialogue. Expect a Question and Answer meeting with the evaluators to clarify your presentation and provide that "two-way" dialogue.

---

[1] *https://www.acquisition.gov/content/15102-oral-presentations*

FAR 15.102(c) provides even greater flexibility in the use of oral presentations. "(c) Information pertaining to areas such as an offeror's capability, past performance, work plans or approaches, staffing resources, transition plans, or sample tasks (or other types of tests) may be suitable for oral presentations." Thus, any or all components of the vendor's technical response can be satisfied through an oral presentation. Contracting Officers are being encouraged to allow oral presentations to replace written proposal responses wherever possible. In accordance with FAR 15.102(c), the Oral presentation is sufficient as an evaluation factor. Expect to see creative acquisitions strategies that streamline the evaluation process through comparative evaluation driven by on-the-spot, consensus. Oral presentations are quickly becoming a "go-to" method to express your proposed content in response to solicitation requirements.

The Rules of the Game – The acquisition team cannot guarantee who wrote the written proposal response but can insist on having a dialogue with the contractor's management team and key personnel. The subtle truth about Orals is that it provides Source Selection the ability to assess the leadership qualities of your Program Manager, the competency of your Key Personnel, how well they work together as a team, and how well your Program Manager and Key Personnel will mix with the customer's Program Management team. Orals is a robust platform that adds necessary tactical texture to your service area and operational strategies. Orals allow the customer to see both your Offer Design and those responsible for its execution.

The Individual Role – As the Orals Coach, your job is to identify and assess the individual level of skill in your player then improve their performance. Each player has a different position on the team; they will be individually different and is equally diverse in their presentation style. Prepare the right message aligned with the right messenger. You are working with each individual to ensure that communication, both visual and verbal, is compliant, compelling, and delivered with excellence.

Team Dynamics – Remember the "game!" The customer will be assessing how the management and technical leadership work together. They are placing the success of their program in the hands of the awardee. It is your job to convince Source Selection that you are the absolute best choice. *It is less the story and more how you express that story.* They may already know your Offer Design if a Technical Volume was submitted prior; this is more how each player champions their part of the story, how the team supports each other, comfort with the subject matter, the transition from one topic to another, and overall teamwork. In the Practice chapter, we exhaust the discussion of format, sectionals, dry runs, presentation styles, time awareness, and situational awareness.

The Game Plan – Every game is different. As the Orals Coach, understand the objective(s) of Source Selection. The presentation may be one of the phases in a Down-Select format or part of an overall acquisition strategy. Determine the rules of engagement. What portion of your Offer Design will be the topic for presentation? Who is allowed to make the presentation? Were questions forwarded to your team prior to the presentation date? Will Q&A wait until the end of the Orals presentation or will Source Selection impose "on-the-spot" questions to encourage dialogue? Will caucusing be allowed by the vendor during Q&A? The job of the Orals Coach is to understand what your team is up against and prepare them for the most effective outcome. You have fully equipped the presentation team for this game; it's time to execute the game plan.

With respect to Orals, this axiom has proven itself to be true, time and time again:

"You can win or lose in Orals!"

Your Orals deck may be a required separate volume in the overall proposal package. Some solicitations designate your Orals presentation as your Technical Approach, submitted within and as part of the Technical Volume. Your presentation cannot change from the time of submission; presenting any new information, to include changes to an existing slide can be grounds for disqualification (DQ). At the very least, any changed slide will be thrown out, not evaluated and your overall rating is indicating non-compliance due to the now missing slide.

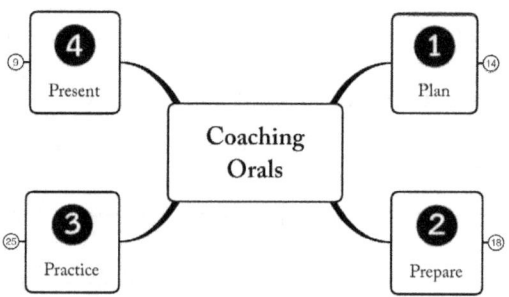

Figure 1 The 4 P's of Coaching Orals

The In Pursuit approach to coaching any oral presentation is based on those familiar "4 P's": Plan, Prepare, Practice, and Present. Although we are tailoring these four processed for acquisition centric presentations and coupled directly to the Business Development Life Cycle, the principles of each process can stand on their own. The same four methods can be leveraged to prepare for any presentation forum.

Plan

Planning for Orals begins in the earlier phases of your pursuit.

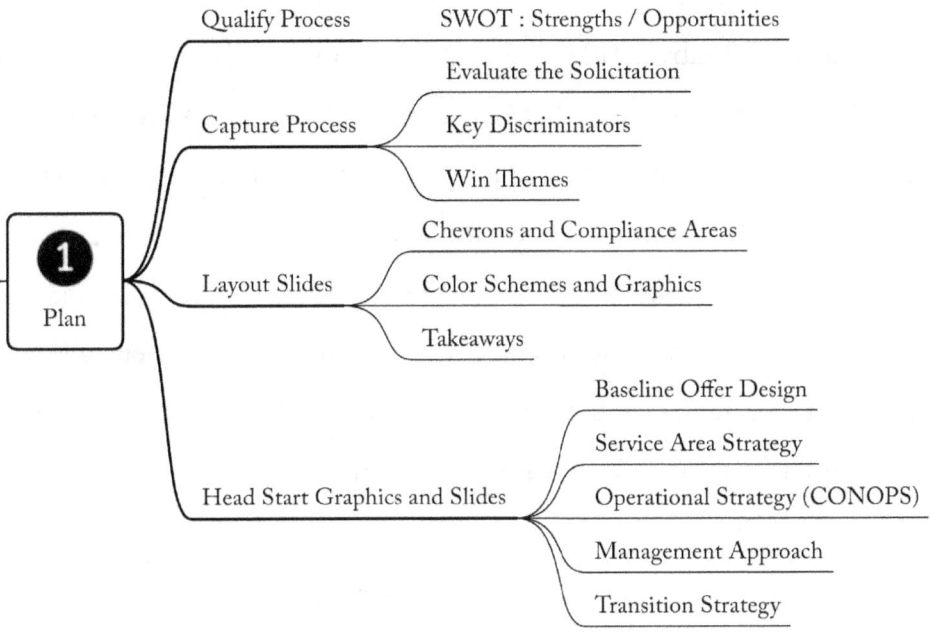

Figure 2 Orals Planning

During the Qualify Process, you identified team strengths and opportunities as a result of your SWOT process. SWOT is an acronym that stands for Strengths, Weaknesses, Opportunities, and Threats. It is a valuable exercise in any decision-making moment that identifies those attributes which may impact the outcome of the decision. Attributes are matrixed between what is Helpful or Harmful and what are Internal to or External from the company's perspective. *Objectivity and honesty must reign during this exercise.*

Curing Capture, you are evaluating the anatomy of the solicitation. If the acquisition follows Title 48 or not, you will look for Section's L and M or their equivalent. Note that GSA Schedule solicitations do not follow Title 48 but have comparable numeric sections. The temptation is to look at Section C, which defines the service or task areas. Most engineers want to address specific service areas. Although necessary for compliance, Section L will advise how the oral response should be structured, and Section M will define evaluation criteria. In short, Section L will provide the compliance criteria for your presentation.

The Capture Process also reveals your Discriminators and Win Themes, those things that separate you from your competition. The Win Strategy is intuitive; it is your strategy to win the pursuit. The Win Theme is the tactical expression of those strategies in a written Proposal or presentation. Embed these same discriminators and win themes into your orals deck. Additionally, your Value Proposition should resonate throughout, both visually and attitudinally by your presenters. If a feature of your proposal is not part of the evaluation criteria per Section M, my advice is not to waste time or real estate in your offer design.

Anatomy of Your Slide – Organizing your orals deck into topic areas is the apparent approach to the presentation order. Not as obvious is how to standardize your motif for each slide to help guide the evaluation team. Chevrons across the slide indicate what section you are presenting at the time. Some designated area on the side to show compliance helps the evaluator map the discussion back to the solicitation. For example, assume this discussion is a required Orals Topic in our presentation to the customer.

In this example RFP, Section C.5.1 instructs the offeror to describe their "Orals Planning" process, and Section L.1.2 instructs the offeror to indicate any relationship of the current Process to all other Processes in the Statement of Work. Although simplistic, the example slide below represents an appropriate slide, presented during the Orals exercise and maintains compliance with both Section C and M of our example solicitation:

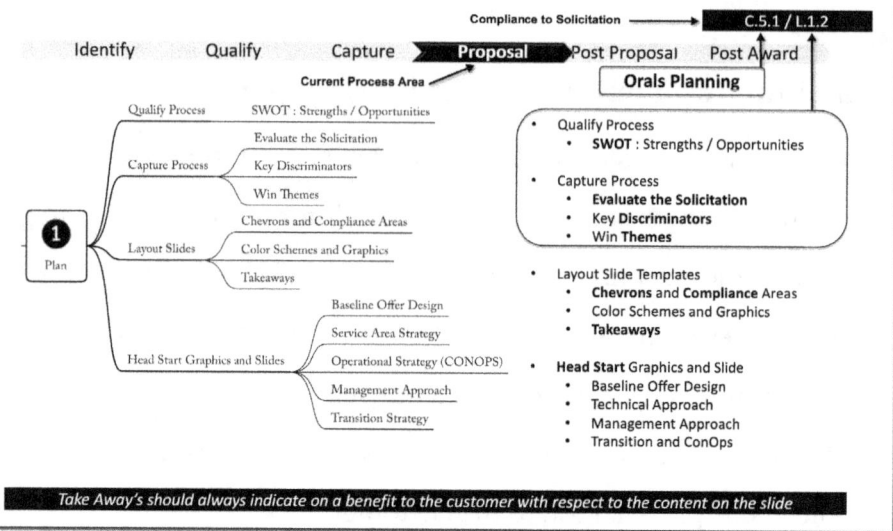

Figure 3 Slide Compliance

The slide's left side satisfies the conceptual mind while the right side of the slide provides raw talking points that the detailed-oriented mind absorbs best. Develop your "takeaway," a final statement highlighting a quantitative benefit of that slide's content to the audience. Not every slide needs a takeaway, but if there is a compelling message, maybe a discriminator in your value proposition, this is an opportunity to communicate it.

Note the "white space" in the side. Try not to fill every inch of the slide with information. Less is more! As the Orals Coach encourage your Key Personnel on how to organize the topic for maximum delivery effectiveness. Engineers, by nature, want completeness in information. This desire for completeness washes over into slides, and too much detail can obscure the story. Unless ... And there is a "but" here ...

If you have ever participated in a FEDSIM acquisition, they want as much information on the side as possible. They are driving for compliance and expect your presentation to be organized per Title 48 Section L (Instructions, Conditions and Notices) and NOT Section C (Technical Task Areas). GSA FEDSIM also requires the offeror to describe proposed methodologies, analytical techniques, tools and industry best practices employed in both the technical and management approaches. Typically, this requirement is satisfied with what is known as the "six pack" slide. This slide will have six boxes labeled, "Challenges", "Methodology", "Analytical Techniques", "Best Practices", "Tools and Resources" and some proof point box called "Corporate Experience".

The orals coach will walk you through the talk track to lift key topics for you to highlight and move on. We'll discuss developing your talk track later. *Know your audience!* Identify essential details for compliance and tutor the presenter to provide compelling dialogue. The slide must be compliant and the presentation, as a whole, is to be compelling.

I want to leave you one final thought on the layout of your slides. Standards remove surprises! Maintaining a standard design for your slides will set the audience's expectations as to what's to come; help them better score your presentation for compliance by training their eye to look at specific areas of your slide for crucial information. I have worked with companies that provide an individual slide toward the front of the deck that indicates color scheme for specific topic boxes, icon legend, and overall layout. The presenter spends 5 seconds of precious time to call the slide to attention and move on with the rest of the presentation.

Much of your graphics were created to support the discussions of your Offer Design, Service Area Strategy, Operational Strategy, Management Approach, and Transition-In Strategy. Graphics used in your written volumes should align with those in your Orals presentation. Ensure that your Graphic's talent understands that all graphics will reside in both places. This assists in the selection of color pallets, fonts, and backgrounds for the best presentation.

Prepare

In preparing your Orals deck, follow the same "Compliance First, Then Compelling" standard. Due to the visual platform which is delivering the message is, focus on Excellence in the presentation. Quality in material and presentation style can make the difference in a win or loss. Each of these three standards has its critical points for discussion.

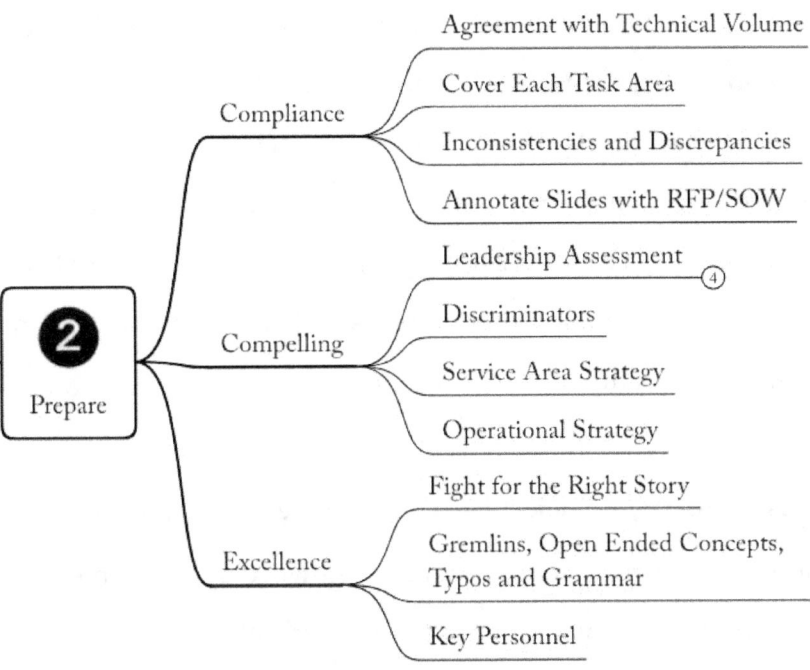

Figure 4 Oral Preparation

Compliance – Enforce the same rigor applied in your Orals deck as with the Technical Volume. The slide presentation must agree with the Technical Volume if evaluated as a separate component to your submission. If the two volumes are independent, your written and visual dialogue must be perfectly in step with each other. Watch for inconsistencies and discrepancies. Contradictions may not necessarily generate clarification questions from the customer and differences may merely cause a slide to be deemed non-compliant. Keep your compliance area in the same section of the slide for quick reference. Source Selection appreciates when you make their job a little more comfortable with references back to their solicitation. The source selection team wants a clean acquisition, and a haphazard deck makes it a time-consuming task to ensure that you get credit for compliance. If your presentation is difficult to score, you may get dinged for quality.

Compelling – Subjective in nature, being considered persuasive depends on the audience. There are, however, three elements to your presentation that will establish your compelling story:

- **Leadership Assessment** – Orals provides Source Selection the opportunity to assess the competency of your Key Personnel, the leadership quality of your Program Manager, teamwork attributes between the PM and KP's and your leadership team's ability to work well with the customer's contract and program office.

- **Discriminators** – Highlight your Win Themes and Discriminators throughout your deck. Tell the story that with your leadership, they can have high confidence you understand the requirement, propose effective solutions, and that you will guarantee success to the execution of the program.

- **Service Area Strategy** – Each Key Personnel present their specific service area. The audience gauges the competence of each KP and how they engage each other and leadership. Convince the audience that your KP is the most compelling candidate to manage their specific service area.

- **Operational Strategy** – The Program Manager presents the strength of your Concept of Operation in meeting the contractual, staffing, and task area compliance. The audience assesses the leadership quality of your PM, how they engage with the KP's and the PM's ability to partner with agency program management team to safeguard the success of the program.

Excellence – Quality of your team is anchored telling a cohesive story, clean slides, and excellence in presentation. As Capture Leadership, fight for the proper story and how its expressed. It is this leadership team, Capture Manager, Proposal Manager, Program Manager, Solutions Architect, and Key Personnel that know best the Offer Design. In the Proposal phase of the pursuit, you introduced new talent to assist in proposal development, who may not necessarily appreciate that story. Make sure that anyone creating collateral for the slide deck grasps the message first, before trying to express it.

The tyranny of the immediate might create the temptation to find shortcuts; especially in collecting collateral for your proposal products. Legacy graphics, management plans, transition plans are all great resources to tap for pre-developed material. Legacy data points, however, introduce "gremlins"; leftovers that can inadvertently become part of your presentation. A good example would be a graphic that was used for a previous proposal and still has the previous customer's name on it. Consider writing a letter to your new love interest. You remembered one you wrote years ago, and you liked how you expressed yourself. You accidentally copy/paste the previous love interest's name into your supposedly new expression of love. ☹ Watch out for those gremlins.

Not as obvious would be leaving too many open-ended concepts which will generate clarification questions from the audience. Each topic should be fully covered and *cleanly closed*. Clarification is good dialogue during an Orals presentation; it has its purpose; too much demand for explanation is an indication of poor delivery. As the Orals Coach, walk through each slide, make sure visual dialogue is clean and complete. Never assume your audience can connect the dots; cognitively connect all the dots for your audience.

Typos and grammar are key quality indicators that deserve your attention. I have heard of debriefs which noted the typos as an indication of the lack of awareness to detail, lowering the score of the company's presentation. Quality in your written platform is critical to a successful Orals presentation.

Equally important is the quality of your presenters. There was a day when companies hired professional Orals talent. Professional talent did not allow the TEB to gauge competencies of the proposed leadership team. As a result, CO's began to enforce that Orals presenters must be Key Personnel, with a Letter of Commitment (LOC) and made this one of the few pass/fail criteria. What do you do when the most competent choice for the KP may be an introvert and struggles to get in front of a crowd? There are two camps in this discussion; 1) pick the best person for the job or 2) pick the best presenter of the topic. I believe your candidate can rally both camps!

In my experience, through practice, you can get any KP to the point that they can comfortably cover their key topic. Your potential customer is looking for competence, not an orator. Also, orals typically have a period in the end for the customer to ask qualifying questions. In some cases, on-the-spot questions surface during the presentation. You want your best talent crafting the perfect answer to those questions. Pick the best person for the job, then coach them into a comfortable and effective presentation.

Practice

Remember that 2X3 learning paradigm from the Business Development Life Cycle? People, in general, are either conceptual or detailed thinkers and absorb information visually, audibly or experientially (also known as tactile learners). The visuals and audibles are intuitive. Tactile or experiential learners are supported by a copy of the deck in front of them, highlighting and making notes in their handwriting. I can always identify tactile learners by their intense scribbling on a copy of a set of notes or slide that were provided by the presenter. Engaging the mind is science, not entertainment. The mind is what we focus on during our orals practice; how to best engage the listener so they can best absorb our message.

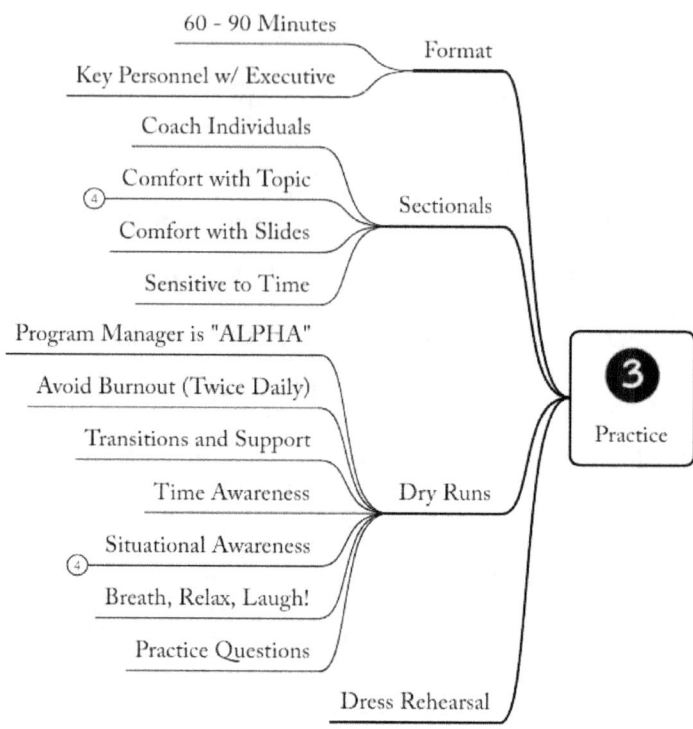

Figure 5 Orals Practice

Format – The duration of your orals session will range based on the requirement of the contracting office. Typically, 60 to 90 minutes for your presentation, a break of 30 minutes for the customer to craft clarification questions and another 60 minutes reserved for Q&A. **FAR 15.102(a)** states, "Oral presentations provide an opportunity for dialogue among the parties." Acquisition teams are being encouraged to include on-the-spot questions to stimulate this two-way dialogue between presenters and evaluators. Evaluators are also introducing scenarios during oral presentations. Do not be surprised to be interrupted with a, "here's one of our issues. How would you address it?"

I have yet to be involved in an Orals exercise where, at some point, we didn't discuss "how much time do we spend on each slide?". Google that question, and you will get as many opinions as there are responses. Some slides are compelling and need a little more time to lavish. Other slides are compliance-centric and the presenter need only to touch the key points and move on.

Understanding the format and time boundaries should always be taken into consideration as you are developing your slides. The Orals Coach has already been working with your Key Personnel in grooming the slides. It's time now to groom the presenter.

Sectionals – I grew up immersed in music. I was singing with my two younger brothers, in church, from the time I was 6; three-part harmony and yes, we were as cute as buttons. As we grew up, we stayed engaged in music. It was in those settings that I gained an appreciation for sectional practice; time set aside to learn our parts. As an Orals Coach, I continue with the technique of sectional practice; working with each until they are comfortable with their "part." I focus on four objectives when working with the team during sectionals:

Coach Individuals – Spend time with each presenter, walking through their section of the deck. Ensure that no slide goes unnoticed. Help with timing, word choice and above all else, compliance. Remember that each presenter is different and may require diverse methods in building their comfort level. As we work with the individual, over time, the presentation smooths out, and you see the desired confidence grow within your presenter. Your presenter needs to work with you as a coach and alone, in front of a mirror, practicing their dialogue, over and over.

Comfort with Topic – Sectionals are designed to get your presenter comfortable with their topic. Extrovert or introvert, anyone with knowledge of a specific subject will engage in conversation and share as long as you stay focused on their area of expertise. Introverts are excellent sharing one-on-one and can be intimidated speaking to a crowd. Inversely, extroverts tend to be anxious one-on-one but thrive in front of a group. Regardless of whether you are coaching introverts or extroverts, there are four types of speech delivery styles employed during a speech or presentation.

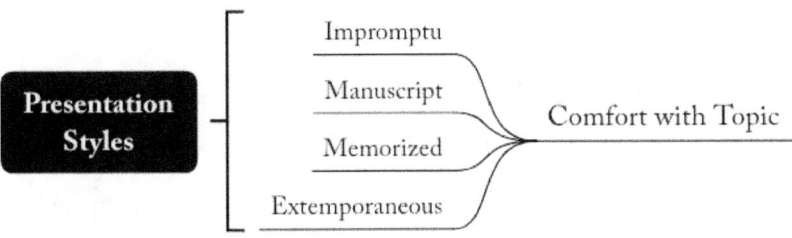

Figure 6 Presentation Styles

Impromptu Presenters rely solely on their knowledge of the subject, their ability to read the audience and quick wit. This type of speaker has tremendous "court sense"; we'll discuss more on situational awareness later. Impromptu speakers tend to drift off script and if they are not careful can lose control of the direction the discussion is going. Impromptu speakers are less sensitive to timeboxes forcing following presenters to adjust their message. This style may be entertaining, and useful, but can be detrimental to a compliant oral presentation if not managed.

Manuscript Presenters read their presentation either from paper or some teleprompter. These types of speakers rarely go "off script" and rarely connect with the audience due to the lack of eye contact. Frankly, I have yet to be part of an Orals event where a manuscript style of presentation was employed.

Memorized Presenters commit the entire presentation to memory. If you have and strong introvert, you may have to coach your presenter to memorize their script queued by the slide change. Memorization has worked in the past with success. I will use memorization to help the fear-prone presenter. We work on timing and body language to help soften the delivery, even memorizing when the speaker looks back to the slide to bring attention to some point of compliance.

Extemporaneous Presenters or "Extemp" are fully comfortable with the topic and work off queues from index cards to guide the dialogue. Extemporaneous means, "without preparation." It is synonymous with "impromptu," but has morphed in definition, over time, to "limited preparation." The heart of this vocal style is knowledge of the topic with little dependence on queues to successfully deliver the message. Replace the index cards with the slide deck, and you have a robust delivery platform which elevates the speaker to expert status on the topic in the minds of the audience.

Extemporaneous is always our goal "mimic" style for our entire presentation team.   Through memorization, topic knowledge, natural ability, strong visuals and practice, our presenters will present themselves as the ultimate experts in their skillset.   I know some admitted introverts who are incredible extemporaneous speakers. This "club" is not exclusive to extroverts. **The key is knowledge and comfort with the topic.**

Comfort with Slides – Regardless of the vocal style, the presentation must follow the slides. At this point, our presenters are so comfortable with the topic, that they only reference the side to point out compliance. Comfort with slides works well with both extroverts and introverts.   The extemporaneous will automatically turn to the slide to support their dialogue. The memorizer knows that now is the time to turn to the slide to and identify a vital compliance point. The impromptu has already chased their third rabbit and is about five slides ahead. ☺ Ouch!

Sensitive to Time – Establish well-defined timeboxes and ensure that each presenter works within their time boundaries. At first, let each presenter go through their presentation. Time it. Pay attention to compliance, but let your athlete see if they can figure out where to save time or expand a bit on their own. Speakers tend to remember their adjustments to their presentation. Coach the tempo where necessary. If they are speaking too fast, slow them down. If they are saying too many filler words, make them conscious of them. Filler words may be "Okay, Uh, Um, Like, totally, literally, clearly." Filler's can also be phrases like, "at the end of the day," "if you ask me," "well, you see," "you know?", "you know what I mean?" and the one that irritates me the most, "in other words." My filler phrase is, "make sense?". I'm working on it.

Dry Runs – Once your sopranos, altos, tenors, and bases have their parts memorized and perfected, it's time to put them together get them to sing as a choir. You will be amazed at how much more work still needs to be done to blend the voices. By definition, dry runs are running through the program from beginning to end and give you, the conductor, the opportunity to begin the blending process of all those voices.

Your KP's can now see each other's presentation and technique. Each will influence the other. Influence is not a bad thing; the convergence of multiple voices into a blended one is your desired outcome. I've seen KP's begin to reference each other during their presentation. As a coach, I enjoyed the comradery within the orals team as they start to draw from and influence each other.

Program Manager is Alpha – I've used the term "alpha" over and over throughout this book series. I'm a believer in leadership, and the lack thereof can appear, if not be, chaotic. In appropriate situations, specific roles take on command. In Orals, and throughout the "Period of Performance," your Program Manager is now the lead role. Leadership is most important during Orals. Orals may be the first time the customer has exposure to your Key Personnel; those who will lead the program to success. Above all, the customer must see and experience your chain of command; well established and in action. Throughout the presentation, practiced here in the dry runs, we develop queues that establish the PM as your leader, balanced with the PM's dependency on the other KP's expertise to ensure the success of the program.

Avoid Burnout – To avoid burnout, I've found it most useful to schedule two dry runs per day. Each day, plan a relaxing lunch with your team. As you get closer to your presentation day, maybe drop your practices to once a day and even put a day between two practice sessions. Also remember that your KP's may have 9-5 jobs and those responsibilities will be weighing on them too.

Transitions and Support – Practice transition from one presenter to the next. I usually have the current presenter introduce the topic and speaker and welcome them to the microphone. A well-coordinated exchange shows knowledge between the team and respect for each other. I even have the two speakers shake hands as they transition positions, with the new presenter saying something to the effect of, "Great job" or "That was awesome." Words of affirmation are incredibly potent, to the presenter and as a positive anchor for your audience. Also, when a team member is presenting, the other team members should practice support by nodding in approval as their teammate works through their material. These are subtle yet powerful messages to the audience that the team is, in fact, a team. In body language, this is called "encoding".

Time Awareness – At this point, you should be timing everyone. Come up with specific queues so that the presenter knows how much time remains for their portion of the deck. It is common for the executive supporting the presentation to play the role of timekeeper. Hand gestures do just fine in letting a speaker know when there is 10-, 5-, 2- and 1-minute(s) left in their timebox. Pick when that queue should be given and stick to it; do not surprise your presenter with a cue that they are not expecting. It can distract the mind and disrupt the flow of the presentation. I've found 5- and 1-minute signals to work best.

Situational Awareness – Some say that "court sense" is innate and cannot be taught. I believe that natural awareness of your surroundings is, in fact, a gift. In athletics, a competent court sense allows an athlete to react based on changes in play. Do not confuse court sense and situational awareness as synonymous. *Court sense is instinctive; Situational Awareness is a discipline!*

The entire team practices situational awareness while one of the team members is actively presenting their portion of the deck; watching the audience, noting or "decoding" non-verbal cues and preparing for their presentation or potential clarification questions at the end of the event.

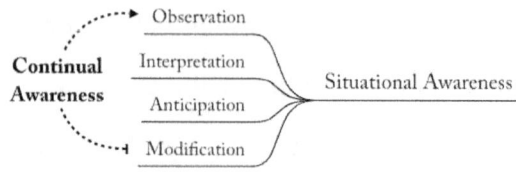

Figure 7 Situational Awareness

Observation – Pay Attention to both the crowd collectively and individuals within the audience. Note who is engaged, who seems bored, who is taking notes and in which topic stimulated the scribbling of notes. Tune into the audience and decode their body language.

Interpretation – Interpretation, or the decoding, of nonverbal communication, is taught, not innate. There are great online resources in learning how to read an audience when giving a presentation. Body language is powerful. Studies suggest that up to 70% of communication is nonverbal. Hand-to-face gesturing, body posture, head tilt, steepling, nodding, tapping their toes, and other evaluation gestures will reveal your audiences' thoughts on the topic. Watch the evaluation team while your bid PM or peer KP is presenting their portion of the deck and interpret what you observe.

Anticipation – Anticipate what the audience is interested in based on your observation and interpretation of the atmosphere. Are the evaluators more involved in your service strategy or how you intend to implement it? There will be visual cues as the topic is presented. It's safe to assume that the TEB has already discussed what they are looking for amongst themselves. Determine where your audience's mind is going and race them to that destination.

Modification – Based on your read of the floor, decide on the appropriate change to your delivery. That adjustment may be as simple as focusing on an individual that may need more eye contact or attention. You may see a TEB member frantically scribbling down notes on a specific topic; a cue that a question may come during Q&A. Commit to your decision and make your modification. Always stay aware of any change in the evaluators' nonverbal cues based on your shift in delivery. Return to observing again and determine if your adjustment was appropriate or not.

Situational Awareness is a perfectly natural process that we do every day in our everyday lives. The goal is to make situational awareness proactive, process driven, purposeful and never reactive.   'Reaction' is a weakness in impromptu speakers; *always reading, always adjusting, never finishing.*

Although situational awareness is for the day of the presentation, it is essential to begin teaching this discipline to your team now. Practice with each other, have your presenters assess the nonverbal cues of their peers while someone is speaking. As a coach, throw in some body language and have your team annotate and adjust accordingly.

Decoding and Encoding non-verbal communications. Court sense may be innate within some individuals but deciphering body language is a skill that can be learned. The key is recognizing and interpreting the language. There are several excellent resources on the topic of body language, and I would encourage the reader to search them out. For the purposes of this book, let's discuss the concept of encoding and decoding body language. Using non-verbal communications to both interpret the audiences level of interest and engage the audiences mind through simple gestures.

Decoding is the process of interpreting non-verbal communications to better understand the message and the messenger.

Encoding is the purposeful use of non-verbal communications to support the dialogue.

Breath, relax and laugh with each other. I love watching outtakes from movies. Some of the greatest moments in Hollywood were picked up off the cutting room floor and compiled for our laughter and pleasure. Although not caught on film, I have experienced some humorous moments practicing orals. I have also been part of a Video Orals Presentation submitted on DVD to the customer. We had some hilarious outtakes and saved them to a "gag reel" for everyone to enjoy. Make practices time for team building.

Practice Questions – Practice clarification questions as a team. Craft up potential questions that you anticipate upon completion of your presentation. Think of areas which may need clarification; introducing new technology or tools are prime fodder for an explanation. The PM will field all questions then caucus or huddle with the entire team, discuss the appropriate response, turn to the audience, and announce who will be responding. Please check with the evaluators to ensure that caucusing is permitted. Opinions of the group huddling are very subjective and vary from evaluator to evaluator. One evaluator may find it lacking in competence, while another sees the value in pursuit of the best answer. Regardless, always have your best of breed responder for that topic answer the question. When your KP is responding to the question, everyone else should be showing interest; nodding in approval. The PM should not be answering every question; sending the message that no one else has a voice.

> **Reflection:** I once, and only once, answered a clarification for one of my leads. This person was an impromptu speaker and tended "chase rabbits" (I know, I'm a rabbit chaser myself). Brilliant as that KP was, I knew this audience well, that they would not appreciate a 10-minute response for a 30-second answer. That audible was appropriate for the moment. There may be other appropriate situations; practice wisdom in calling that rare "audible."

Dress Rehearsal – This is far more than putting on your Sunday best and running through the presentation. Invite new audience members, peer business development talent, other executives, etc. Fresh faces create a new audience. Up until now, your team has been presenting to each other. Now they can tackle some of the nerves of performing to new faces. Your Coach should attempt to simulate the environment as close to the actual presentation as possible. One technique I've used in the past is to tell the team that Oral's will begin promptly at 11 am and make them sit outside the conference room for 15 minutes before starting. Encourage your team to encourage each other! Waiting can be unnerving, but with a little strategy, you can turn that time into productive team building.

Your dress rehearsal is your final run through. At this point, your presentation team should have everything down. Engage in situational awareness and share notes at the end of your rehearsal — practice clarification questions from the mock crowd. Be positive, no more tweaking, have a team lunch, laugh together and send everyone home early. Tomorrow is the Big Day!

Present

The Big Day has arrived for your presentation. Chronologically your presentation is typically scheduled during the Post Proposal phase of the Life Cycle. Note, however, that Orals, may be the core substance of your proposal.

The team should be well rested with sufficient nutrition to fuel the day. The team should be onsite at least an hour ahead of schedule. If everyone is early, you successfully removed one stressor to the day for everyone.

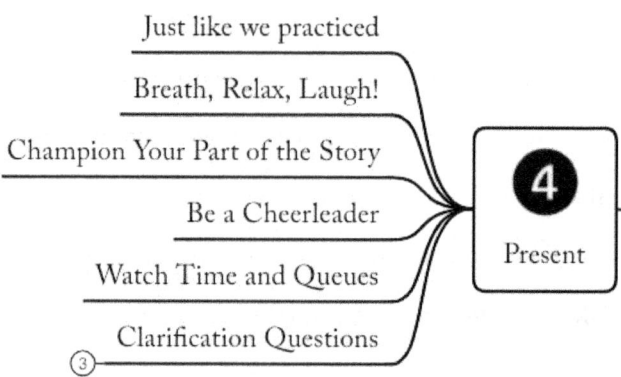

Figure 8 Orals Presentation

To the Program Manager, you will hear this over and over again; at this time, you are "Alpha." The evaluators are interested in the competency of your Key Personnel, but they are keenly interested in your ability to run the program, work well with your team and partner with the customer to achieve success. You will most likely be the first to present after some executive "hello." It's up to you to set the expectations of both the evaluating audience and your team.

Reflection: I was the Bid PM for a large software engineering deal. We were the prime, and my business partner and friend was the executive kicking off Orals. He went on about being excited to be there, introducing our partners, our long-lasting partnership with the customer, then went into this dialogue of how long he knew me, trusted me and that I was more than an employee, I was one of his closest friends. After the introduction, I stood up and opened with, *"Wow! I wonder if I can get added to his 'will' along with his kids!"*. The audience laughed, and we moved on. We were able to set the tone for the morning, everyone relaxed, and it was an enjoyable and productive presentation.

Just like we practiced – At this point, your team should be on automatic pilot. I always encourage the team with, "You got this … just like we practiced … Now go get 'em!". Orals are usually straightforward, and the Contracting Office will run the event just as defined in the solicitation. If you practiced accordingly, then the statement, "Just like we practiced" is the truth.

Breath, Relax, Laugh! – Keep up that upbeat attitude throughout the presentation. Everyone should maintain an atmosphere of confidence and comfort.

Champion Your Part of the Story – Remember the purpose of Orals as you present your specific service area. The goal is to convince the audience that you are the most compelling candidate to ensure the success in your leadership role. Champion your presentation and convince the audience that there is a significant risk if you are not the technical lead for this task area.

Be a Cheerleader – Body language does not always have to be involuntary. Purposeful body language, "encoding", sends a strong message to both your peer KP who is presenting and the audience. Your positive nonverbal signals, nods of approval and positive body posture that shows you are entirely engaged help establish a receptive atmosphere that the audience will tune in.

Mirroring is a powerful non-verbal bonding mechanism that is innate in most humans. Usually oblivious to our natural mimicking gestures of the person of interest, notice ... how we dress, how we walk and talk, the longer couples are together will even begin to mimic each other's facial expressions and appear to begin to look like each other. Spend some time in the office and decode mirroring within the company's workforce. Mirroring is a genetic mechanism used to establish rapport. However, any non-verbal gesture can also be cognitive, purposefully encoded to send a message. Mirroring can be a powerful strategy when a team is giving a presentation. During the orals presentation, as the presenter drives home a core point, have that presenter make a gesture, a thumbs up, a fist shake of approval, or a head nod, then have the rest of the team, on que, mimic the movement. This sends a powerful message that the team is in agreement.

> **Reflection:** Once, and unexpected, I saw one of my KP's finish a challenging topic, turned to the Bid PM and asked, "How was that, Boss?". The PM responded "Perfect!". What a powerful and positive exchange! The PM sent a powerful message to both the audience and to the rest of the team. That truly was a *perfect* moment in Orals history!

Watch Time and Queues – During your dry runs and dress rehearsal, you identified who will be your time monitor. Remember, just like we practiced; same cues; **no surprises**.

Clarification Questions – Once the presentation concludes, the team will retreat for approximately 30 minutes while the TEB crafts up clarification questions. Take this time to review everyone's situational awareness notes. Maybe start a nickel pool based on who figured out what clarification question(s) will be asked when you return to the evaluators.

When you return to the presentation area, have the team take the same seats as before and await the questions. Most likely, the CO will ask the question. Listen carefully, and if there is any confusion, the PM should ask to have the clarification request explained. The CO will usually turn to the author of the question to indicate what needs further explanation; upon which, you can award nickel bet.

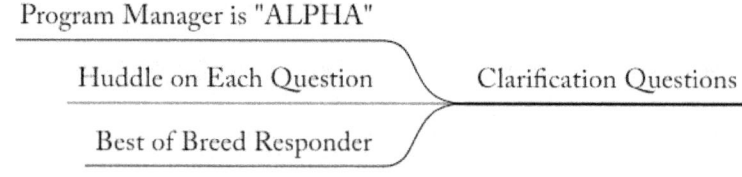

Figure 9 Clarification Questions

Regardless of how confident you are in who will answer the question, and if caucusing is allowed, the PM states, "I would like to discuss this with my team," wait for confirmation from the CO and huddle. Give your responder time to think, allow for team interjection and discussion. Then turn back to the evaluation team and state who will be responding. Deferring to the KP shows PM leadership and dependence on their technical genius to provide the best response.

Once orals are completed, thank the members of the source selection for allowing you the privilege of presenting with your team and graciously retreat to some common area. Congratulate each other as you leave the presentation area, stay positive and leave your audience with a good sense of accomplishment

Conclusion

The FAR gives tremendous flexibility to Contracting Officers is developing their acquisition strategies. We stated that **FAR 15.102(c)** clearly states that oral presentations can sufficiently replace the written responses for capabilities, past performances, management plans, staffing approaches and resources, transition plans and service area approaches to task areas. The FAR also provides flexibility to the evaluation team to score your evaluation immediately after your presentation through confidence ratings, comparative evaluations, and on-the-spot consensus evaluation. Acquisition professionals are discovering tremendous latitude within these regulation(s). With the use of Oral Presentations, Technical Challenges, Product Demonstrations and Down Select formats, to name a few, Contracting Officers are streamlining the solicitation process, minimizing time to award, reducing protests and saving overall acquisition spend. Oral presentations expose the knowledge of management and technical leadership in the stated requirements. If compliant, competent, and compelling, the customer's confidence in your team rises. Your goal is to have that confidence rise above the rest in the competitive landscape.

So, remember that axiom that has proven itself to be true, time and time again:

"You can win or lose in Orals!"

Through excellence in planning, preparing and practicing your message will be presented with competence, confidence and enthusiasm.